HEROES AND OUTLAWS
OF THE OLD WEST

by
Shane Edwards

SANTA MONICA PRESS
P.O. Box 1076
Santa Monica, CA 90406-1076
Printed in the United States
All Rights Reserved

This book may not be reproduced
in whole or in part or in any
form or format without written
permission of the publisher

©1993 SANTA MONICA PRESS

CONTENTS

IRA ATEN

Born: Cairo, Illinois, 1863
Died: Burlingame, California, 1953

When Ira Aten was still very young, his family moved to Round Rock, Texas. His father was a minister who ran a private farm. As Ira grew older, he took to shooting his father's rifle, and before long he became an excellent shot. He had such a good reputation around town that he was encouraged by friends to join the Texas Rangers when he was twenty.

Aten's jurisdiction was over the border between the U.S. and Mexico. In 1884 he single-handedly captured two cattle rustlers who were trying to cross the border in order to escape U.S. law. The rustlers were able to shoot both of his partners, but he wounded the outlaws and took them into custody. He was promoted to corporal for his actions.

In 1887, Aten was involved in a manhunt for an outlaw named Judd Roberts. Roberts had escaped from a jail in Texas before he could be tried for murder. Aten tracked him across three counties, finally encountering him in Williamson County. Aten attacked Roberts by surprise, shooting him in the arm, but the outlaw managed to escape. Aten stayed on his trail, however, and after two months he finally caught up with the man. Aten hid in the ranch of a man known to be a rival of Roberts. One night, Roberts approached, presumably to start a fight with the rancher. Aten revealed himself and again wounded Roberts, but the outlaw was again able to escape. One month later, Aten finally managed to catch up with his prey one last time, in the Texas Panhandle. Roberts had gone to visit a woman, and the Texas Ranger waited outside of her home. Roberts emerged with his gun drawn, so Aten shot him dead.

Aten's career in law enforcement continued to flourish. After retiring from the Texas Rangers, he became the sheriff of several counties, some of which were notorious for their criminal elements. In 1904 he moved to California in order to lead a more placid life with his family. He died in 1953.

CLINT BARKLEY

Born: Unknown
Died: Unknown

In 1873, Clint Barkley found himself accused of a murder he did not commit. He changed his name to Bill Bowen and ran away to a town called Lampasas, Texas. He gained employment with the notorious Horrell brothers, working at their cattle ranch in exchange for food and shelter. They were all too happy to oblige; their hatred for law and order led them to love outlaws such as Barkley.

A few months after settling into his new life in Lampasas, state lawmen finally found his trail and came to arrest him. The Horrells decided that they had to help defend their new friend, so they hid Barkley in a local saloon. When the lawmen discovered where Barkley was hiding, the Horrells shot them dead. Two of the Horrells were injured, however, and they were dragged off to jail by a local Marshal.

Grateful to his bosses for their protection, Barkley agreed to help break the two men out of jail. He smashed down the jail door with a sledgehammer while the Horrells covered him with their rifles. Barkley was slightly wounded by a gunshot from a local do-gooder, but he did not cease in his efforts until the men had been freed.

Barkley and the Horrells escaped to New Mexico, and there they lived for four years. They were involved in various gunfights and robberies, but they tried to keep as low a profile as possible. They returned to Lampasas in 1877, and they quickly became embroiled in a feud with a rancher named Higgins after they tried to steal some of his cattle.

A few weeks after the feud began, several of the Horrell brothers began shooting at some of the Higgins brothers in the middle of the town square. The Higgins returned fire, and the gunfight quickly escalated. Townspeople were forced to run from the streets in order to protect themselves. The following month, Higgins hired fourteen gunmen to accompany him on an attack on the Horrell household. Higgins pinned them down in the house for two days, but they fought back so strongly that their attacker eventually had to give up and return home.

By this time, Barkley realized he had had enough of the Horrells. He secretly ran away from them one night, and eventually faded into anonymity.

BLACK BART

Born: Unknown
Died: Unknown

The Wells Fargo stagecoach was a staple of transportation in the Old West. It ran frequently, usually with several passengers aboard, and always with an armed escort. It was generally considered a fairly dangerous way to travel, as the coach had to pass through treacherous and lawless areas between stops. In 1875, a man wearing a flour sack on his head held up the stagecoach somewhere in Calaveras County, in Northern California. The man carried a double-barrel shotgun, and he gave polite orders to his gang, who were apparently hiding behind the boulders and other obstructions in the terrain. The driver could not see the men, but he could see their rifle barrels. The man in the sack took the Wells Fargo money box, but he did not steal from any of the passengers.

When the stage reached its destination, the driver wired Wells Fargo. The bank dispatched its private police force to the scene of the crime. They discovered that the rifle barrels were merely propped-up sticks, and they found a poem on the ground, apparently written by the bandit. The poem was signed, "Black Bart, PO-8." They could turn up no leads, however, so they decided to detain the driver for questioning. But he was released when another stage was robbed by a man fitting Black Bart's description the following week. The private police investigated this crime also, and they found another poem signed by Black Bart. No expense was spared in trying to catch the bandit; although he had only stolen $700, Wells Fargo did not want other outlaws getting any ideas into their heads. The bank hired some of the best criminal investigators of the time, and they even posted an $800 reward.

The hold-ups stopped, and Wells Fargo was happy, even though they had never caught their man. But five months later, Black Bart struck yet again. Investigators found another poem, and they discovered that over $1000 had been stolen. They scoured the countryside looking for witnesses, and they eventually found a farmer who had noticed a distinguished looking stranger with sideburns a few days earlier. But other locals claimed that the farmer to whom the inspectors had spoken was crazy, so the private policemen found themselves stumped.

Six months later, Black Bart robbed another stage. And six months after that, he robbed another. This continued for several years, the bandit taking in many thousands of dollars. Wells Fargo began placing detectives in strategic locations along the routes, so they could quickly find the bandit's trail. Their plan was a success; one of the detectives was able to find a stockpile of evidence near a hold-up sight; one piece of evidence, a handkerchief, had a laundry mark inscribed on it. The detectives did some research, and they traced the mark to a laundry in San Francisco. After questioning the proprietor, they discovered that the handkerchief belonged to a Mr. C.E. Bolton. Bolton was arrested, and after many weeks of interrogation he finally confessed. Because he gave back almost all of the money he had stolen — he had spent just $200 of it — he only went to jail for a few years.

After Bolton was released from jail, Black Bart struck again twice. Police tried to track him down, but they were unable to. It seems that Bolton was an alias, and they did not even know where to start looking for the bandit with no name.

CHEROKEE BILL

Born: Fort Concho, Texas, 1876
Died: Fort Smith, Arkansas, 1896

Crawford Goldsby was the victim of racism at an early age, probably triggering the violence within him that would consume his later years. He was part Native American, part Black, part Mexican, and part White; his nickname was Cherokee Bill. His family life was made even more traumatic by the fact that his parents separated when he was very young, probably due to his father's excessive drinking.

At the age of eighteen, Cherokee Bill got into his first gunfight. He went to a dance in Fort Gibson, Oklahoma, with several of his friends. Over the course of the evening, he began arguing with a Black man. After an hour or so, the argument progressed to a fist fight, and when Bill began to lose, it became a gunfight. Bill shot his opponent and left town that night.

A few months later, Cherokee Bill be-friended two brothers named Bill and Jim

Cook. He was fiercely loyal to them, as they were the first true friends he had ever had. One day a sheriff came to arrest the Cook brothers for stealing some horses, and rather than see his friends go to jail, Cherokee Bill shot the lawman. The Cooks were grateful to him, so they indoctrinated him into their gang. He joined them in numerous robberies and gunfights.

That same year, Bill learned that his sister had been beaten by her husband. He followed his brother-in-law, who had fled after learning that Bill was coming after him. Several days later, Bill finally caught up with the man and shot him to death.

Cherokee Bill was arrested and sentenced to death for killing a train conductor several months later, but he was rescued by the Cook gang. A year later, however, he was caught once again, and Judge Isaac Parker — "the hanging judge" — sentenced him to be hanged by the neck. That night he killed one of the prison guards, who happened to have four children. Judge Parker was so enraged by this action that he had Bill hanged the very next day.

TEXAS BILLY

Born: Knottingley, England, 1845
Died: Laredo, Texas, 1888

William Thompson was the son of an alcoholic. His father moved from England to Texas, for unknown reasons, while William was very young. He employed himself by catching fish, and William had to sell them in the streets in order for the family to make ends meet.

William adopted the nickname "Texas Billy." He joined the Second Regiment of Texas Mounted Rifles during the Civil War, but he often avoided his duties in order to hold poker games with other soldiers. In 1868 he went to a brothel with one of his fellow soldiers during a three-day leave. The two men got into a drunken fight later that night, and Billy soon realized that he had killed his friend. Billy managed to dodge all of the search parties that were sent out after him, and he fled the state.

By 1872, Billy had become a card dealer in

Abilene. He kept a low profile and tried not to draw any undue attention to himself, in hopes that no one would learn of his past. But his sedate life was shattered when he accidentally killed the local sheriff. One night, while in a drunken stupor, he heard that one of his friends was involved in a brawl. He picked up his shot gun and went to see if he could help in any way, but in his drunkenness he accidentally fired the gun, nearly shooting a passing couple. He then fired another shot, this time hitting the sheriff, who happened to be his best friend. He was forced to flee from town.

Three years later he was apprehended by Texas Rangers as a suspected cattle rustler. When the Rangers realized who they had in custody, they returned him to Kansas in order to stand trial for the sheriff's murder. He was acquitted.

In 1880 Billy was severely wounded in a gunfight. He was saved by Bat Masterson of Dodge City, an old friend. Bat took him to Dodge City where he recovered from his wounds, but Billy was killed eight years later in a gunfight in Laredo, Texas.

CHARLIE BOWDRE

Born: Mississippi or Tennessee, 1859
Died: Stinking Springs, New Mexico, 1880

Not much is known of Charlie Bowdre prior to his arrival in Lincoln County, New Mexico. He was a member of Billy the Kid's gang, and he fought during the Lincoln County War. He was accused of many crimes, and he was guilty of most of them.

One day in 1877, he got drunk with a friend and began firing bullets into a store. Inside the store was a rancher who had recently fired Bowdre for suspected cattle rustling. By the time the two drunken men were through, very little was left of the facade of the store, but amazingly no one inside was hurt. Not realizing this, the two went off to a bar. They were then confronted by the local sheriff, beaten over the heads with pistols, and carted off to jail.

The following year, in a fierce battle of the Lincoln County War, Bowdre narrowly escaped death. A man named Buckshot Roberts, who was a member of the faction that fought against Bowdre and his friends, accidentally rode into their territory. Bowdre ordered him to surrender, but Buckshot refused. The two men proceeded to shoot at each other. Bowdre blew a large hole through Buckshot's chest, but he was then hit in the midriff by a bullet that knocked him to the ground. Somehow, Buckshot Roberts managed to crawl for cover, killing two of Bowdre's allies on the way. Roberts was injured so badly, however, that he died shortly thereafter. Bowdre revived several moments later and realized that he had not been injured at all; the bullet had bounced off a metal plate in his belt. He limped to safety.

Bowdre realized that his life as an outlaw would someday catch up with him. When he discovered that Pat Garrett was hunting Billy the Kid, Bowdre pleaded with the lawman to be exonerated. Garrett refused, and Bowdre was forced to join Billy on his flight from the law. On December 23, Pat Garrett managed to discover their hideout in Stinking Springs. After the dust settled from a horrific shoot-out, Bowdre was found dead.

JACK L. BRIDGES

Born: Maine, 1838
Died: Unknown

The United States census of 1870 states that Jack Bridges was born at sea, but most historians agree that he was probably born in Maine, some time around 1830. He somehow found his way to the West, however, and he spent at least fifteen years of his life in Kansas. He was a law officer during most of that time.

In 1869, Bridges was appointed Deputy U.S. Marshal. He lived in Wichita, Kansas at that time. Two years later, a cattle rustler named J. E. Ledford moved into town with his new bride. Ledford and Bridges were old rivals, and they had engaged in several fist fights over the years. Bridges decided to arrest the outlaw, and he approached the man's house in the dead of night with a posse of twenty-five men. Bridges noticed some movement in the lawn outside, over by the outhouse, and he went to investigate. Ledford suddenly jumped out of the outhouse, firing his handgun maniacally at the lawman. Bridges and his posse returned Ledford's fire, killing the rustler in a hail of bullets. Bridges received serious wounds to his chest during the gunfight, and he had to be treated in a nearby military hospital. He then traveled back to Maine to convalesce for many months.

Upon returning to Kansas, he got married to the woman he had been seeing prior to his injury. In 1882, he moved to Dodge City and became the local Marshal. He was involved in few incidents while at Dodge, except for a brief feud with an outlaw named Luke Short. When that feud came to an end, Bill Tilghman took over the post of Marshal. Bridges moved away with his wife, and he was never heard from again.

WILLIAM L. BROOKS

Born: Unknown
Died: Wellington, Kansas, 1874

Not much is known of William Brooks' life prior to 1872. He was probably a gunfighter, and he was definitely a stage driver, but no one knows where or when he was born. He was the first Marshal ever elected in the town of Newton, Kansas, an honor he had earned from his reliability as a stage driver.

Brooks was wounded very badly in a gunfight just several months after he took office, however, and he was forced to resign. Several cowboys from Texas had been beating up an innocent man, so the Marshal had ordered them out of town. On their way out, they had opened fire on him. He tried to stop them, but he was injured too badly to begin a pursuit. He then moved to Dodge City and became a buffalo hunter after convalescing for many months.

Brooks was involved in two gunfights in

Dodge City toward the end of 1872. The first was the result of an ongoing argument he had with an employee of the local train station. The two men fired at each other simultaneously. Both shots missed their marks, but Brooks' bullet ricocheted off an innocent bystander and killed the train worker. Five days later, he shot a saloon-keeper through an open window. The two men had been quarreling for weeks prior to the incident. No action was taken against Brooks on either occasion.

By 1874, Brooks had become a horse thief in Caldwell, Kansas. He was working for a stage company that was trying to drive another stage company out of the area. A posse was organized to capture him. They found him hiding out with two other suspects several hours later, and he was promptly arrested. He was never brought to trial, however, as he was lynched that night by an angry mob.

BUTCH CASSIDY

Born: Beaver, Utah, 1866
Died: Spangle, Washington, 1937

Robert Leroy Parker was a descendant of some of the original Mormon settlers of Utah. His parents ran a general store, but they moved the family to a ranch shortly after he was born. He had twelve brothers and sisters. The ranch was located in an area that was full of cattle rustlers, and as Robert grew older he fell in with a young outlaw named Mike Cassidy. Mike taught him how to ride and shoot, and Robert soon joined the ranks of cattle thieves.

The illegal activities of this gang grew in scope over the next few years. They went from a bunch of kids who stole livestock to a group of men who robbed banks and trains. Robert decided to adopt the alias George Cassidy, but he became known to his friends as Butch after working as a butcher for several months.

In the 1880s, Butch Cassidy tried to leave

behind his life of crime. He worked as a cowboy for over five years, but he somehow managed to fall in with a crowd of cattle rustlers again. He became an active rustler in the area, and by 1892 the law had caught up with him. He sat in jail until 1896, at which point he resumed his career as an outlaw.

His years in jail had given Butch many ideas. He decided to form the most notorious gang conceivable, its ranks filled with murderers and thieves, and named it the Wild Bunch. His right-hand-man was named Harry Longabaugh, otherwise known as the Sundance Kid. The two men orchestrated some of the most daring train and bank robberies of the time, and they always lived it up after a job. Occasionally they were forced to go into hiding, becoming sailors on steamships. By 1902, Butch's reputation had grown too big for its own good. He was known to almost every lawman in the Old West, not to mention by many people across the country who were desperate for a folk hero. In order to evade the law, he was forced to flee the country with Sundance, who brought his mistress with him.

The two went their separate ways for some time. Sundance moved to South America, while Butch spent a few months in England and the Canary Islands. They met up again in Argentina and opened a ranch. But the life of law-abiding citizens did not sit well with them, so they moved to Bolivia and began robbing trains. They were captured by Bolivian soldiers in 1908, and Sundance was killed. Butch escaped and returned to America.

He made a home for himself in Iowa and married a pretty young woman. She had bad asthma, however, so the couple moved West, where the air was purer. Butch ran a small business, but he went broke at the start of the Great Depression. He tried to publish his autobiography shortly thereafter, but no one would buy it. He died of cancer in 1937.

DAN CLIFTON

Born: Unknown
Died: Checotah, Oklahoma, 1897

No one knows much about Dan Clifton prior to the 1890s. But from the year 1890 until his death in 1897, he made it clear to lawmen that he was an outlaw to be feared. Prior to the 1890's he had probably been a cattle thief, but that was nothing compared to the violent crimes in which he participated during the last decade of his life.

In 1891, Clifton joined the "Oklahombres," a gang of vicious outlaws organized by Bill Doolin. The following year, he accidentally ran into Lafe Shadley, a lawman who had been hunting him. The two began firing at each other, and Clifton was badly wounded in the neck, resulting in a horrible scar. Amazingly, he was able to flee the scene. The following year, he was pinned down by a posse in a hotel in Ingalls, Oklahoma with Bill Doolin. The two men shot their way out, killing and wounding many in the posse, until they finally found some horses and rode to freedom.

Clifton was involved in several bank robberies with Doolin's gang after that, all of which involved massive amounts of gunplay. He was wounded several times during these robberies, but no wound compared to the one he had received from Lafe Shadley. In 1896, he was captured by lawman Heck Thomas and his posse, and he was sent to jail along with several other members of Doolin's gang. However, he bribed a guard in order to be set free a few months after he was imprisoned, and he escaped to freedom with ten or twelve other convicts.

In 1897, a posse led by Marshals George Lawson and William Bussey tracked Clifton down on a farm in Checotah, Oklahoma. They fired several warning shots at him, but he responded by shooting one of the members of the posse. They began shooting at him for real this time, and he was hit in the side, thrown from his horse and began running away. Injured and on foot, the posse quickly caught up with him and shot him in the back.

GEORGE WASHINGTON COE

Born: Brighton, Iowa, 1856
Died: Lincoln, New Mexico, 1941

George Coe's father was a veteran of the Civil War. That conflict had left the man emotionally scarred. When his father returned home, George still had to rely mostly on his mother, as the man seemed distant most of the time. The family moved to a small home in Missouri, where the climate agreed with his father's health.

In 1874, George left home and went to work for his cousin in New Mexico. Four years later, Coe had amassed enough money to lease his own ranch in Lincoln County. He could not have picked a worse time to make an investment. Lincoln County was virtually lawless due to local feuds, and on many occasions the sheriff threatened to take his land away from him. Coe defiantly protected his property, however, antagonizing the local "law enforcement" officers greatly. On one occasion he was arrested by the sheriff and sent to jail for no reason. He was then tortured by local deputies. He was finally released several weeks later, without ever having stood trial.

Coe became angry after that. He shot at almost anyone who tried to approach his land, wounding several deputies, and killing several others. He became a member of a gang known as the Regulators, which fought bitterly in the Lincoln County War, trying to protect the lives and property of innocent locals.

The war eventually came to an end, and Coe moved to San Juan County. He had some minor trouble with the law there, but he was simply regarded as stubborn. Most people in the area seemed to like him, and he married a young woman who had spent her whole life there. A few years later he returned to Lincoln County and bought a ranch and a general store. After finding religion, he spent many peaceful years in his home with his family. He died in 1941.

LEWIS S. DELONY

Born: Clinton, Texas, 1857
Died: Unknown

Delony was the son of one of the earliest members of the Texas Rangers. His father was a soldier in both the Mexican War and the Civil War. He settled down to a life in DeWitt County, Texas, laboring as a school teacher and a tax assessor for the county. But the tranquil life that he had hoped for in order to raise his children was shattered when a bitter feud broke out between two rival families. Instead of growing up in a sheltered environment, Lewis Delony grew up carrying a pistol with him to school every day of his childhood.

By the age of fourteen, Lewis had tired of his violent home, so he left to work at various odd jobs in Mississippi. He then returned to the town of Clinton, Texas. He became a store clerk, and he was well respected for his integrity and disciplined attitude. He was soon asked to become the deputy sheriff of the town, and he eagerly accepted the position. He did not want to let Clinton become a violent town like the one in which he had been raised.

In 1877, Delony followed in his father's footsteps and became a Texas Ranger. One of his most important duties was to prevent smuggling along the U.S.-Mexican border. In 1879, he ran into a smuggler who was hastily making his way from a saloon. The outlaw had just fired several shots at a local deputy, and he was attempting to escape. Delony killed the man's horse with a shot-gun, but the outlaw was able to find cover and escape to freedom.

Three years later, Delony was called to break up a fight in a dance hall. When he arrived, he found that a man had killed a deputy and a Mexican woman who had been dancing together. A gunfight ensued in which Delony shot the man in the chest. The man survived the incident, and he was later acquitted of the charges against him by a local court. In 1887, Delony married a beautiful young woman. He retired from his life of law enforcement, and he finally settled down to the tranquil home of which he had always dreamed.

BILL DOOLIN

Born: Johnson County, Arkansas, 1858
Died: Lawson, Oklahoma, 1896

Bill Doolin's earliest years were very quiet. His father was a farmer, so young Bill grew up plowing fields and milking cows. But at the age of twenty-three, Doolin decided that he had had enough of his tranquil life, and he ran away to the lawless territory of Oklahoma. He was employed as a cowboy on a large ranch for a few years, but after a while he was seduced into a life of crime by the notorious Dalton gang. He soon found himself robbing trains and banks, and having the time of his life. Doolin managed to escape when the law caught up with the Daltons, and he went on to form his own gang, named the "Oklahombres."

In 1893, while Doolin and his gang were returning from a train robbery, they were ambushed by Chris Madsen and his posse. A violent shoot-out occurred, resulting in Bill Doolin's foot being shattered by a bullet. The outlaws were able to escape, however, and for the next two years, the Oklahombres were involved in many bank robberies and shoot-outs. In 1895, while robbing a bank, Doolin was wounded slightly in the head by a bullet. The robbery had gone sour, and one of the guards had tried to fight back.

By 1896, the people of Oklahoma decided that they had had enough of Bill Doolin and his gang. Three of the state's greatest lawmen banded together in order to catch the outlaws. Chris Madsen, Bill Tilghman, and Heck Thomas were known as the "Three Guardsman." They pursued the gang for almost a year before tracking Doolin down at a health spa where he was recovering from an illness. On the way to trial, however, Doolin escaped.

It wasn't long before the "Three Guardsmen" discovered his hideout. They waited for him for weeks. When Doolin decided that the search for him must finally have been called off, he emerged and was greeted by a hail of gunfire. He was killed by a shotgun shell that ripped over twenty holes in his chest.

WYATT EARP

Born: Monmouth, Illinois, 1848
Died: Los Angeles, California, 1929

Named after Colonel Wyatt Berry Stapp, under whom his father had served in the Mexican War, young Wyatt was raised in Pella, Iowa. He had four brothers, a sister, and a half-brother from his father's prior marriage. He was raised with the dream of settling in California, but illness and the Civil War prevented the family from daring such a move. Although his parents, Nicholas and Virginia, had been born in Virginia, they objected to secession by the South. Nicholas and three of his sons joined the U.S. Army. Wyatt wanted to join, but he was too young. He ran away to enlist elsewhere in Iowa, but he was discovered and sent back home.

In 1864 the family attempted to move West. They got as far as Wyoming, where they were attacked by a Sioux war party, claiming the life of one of Wyatt's brothers. In December they finally reached San Bernardino, California, but Wyatt soon grew weary of the calm lifestyle there. He ran off and became a successful stage coach driver, shuttling valuable goods along the dangerous and unpatrolled routes between Arizona, Utah, and California.

This employment kept him occupied for some time, and he earned a courageous reputation for himself, but in 1875 he decided to move to Wichita, Kansas. He was hired as a policeman, but he lost his job after just one year for getting into a fight in the streets. Sources differ as to the cause of the brawl, but many believe Earp was attempting to stop a businessman from beating his hired hand to death. Earp moved to Dodge City and became an assistant Marshal. Contrary to popular belief, he never became full Marshal. Further contrary to popular belief, Dodge City was a placid town. There had only been a few murders, and there were rarely more than three or four dozen court cases per year.

Earp quit after a year so that he could join the gold rush, but luck was not with him, and he soon returned to his job. He was promptly fired, however, for getting into a fight with a dance hall girl. In 1879 he became deputy sheriff of Tombstone, Arizona. He appointed his three brothers, along with the notorious Doc Holliday, as his Marshal and deputies. The five men got into the famed Gunfight at the OK Corral in 1881 when their feud with the dreaded Clanton gang reached a fever pitch. The Earps won the gunfight — barely. While acquitted for acting in the line of duty, they were criticized for their actions and subsequently forced to leave town.

Wyatt decided to spend the rest of his days traveling. He ran a saloon in Alaska for four years during the Yukon gold rush. In 1902 he returned to the warmth of the Southwest, opening another saloon in Tonopah, Nevada. He eventually returned to the quiet life in California and died in 1929, at the age of eighty.

ROBERT FORD

Born: 1861
Died: Creede, Colorado, 1892

Robert Ford was dedicated to his parents, refusing to leave home until the age of twenty. He even accompanied them when they moved to Missouri in 1879. Ford was an upstanding young man, and he seemed destined to become a law abiding citizen — until his brother Charlie corrupted him. Charlie was a member of Jesse James' gang, and he occasionally dragged Robert along with him on holdups.

In 1882, at the urging of Charlie, Robert hid two members of the James gang in the home of his widowed sister. One morning while at breakfast, the two men began arguing with each other for no apparent reason. Ford tried to break up the fight, but the two outlaws pushed him aside and began firing at each other. Ford realized that he would have to end the fight quickly in order not to draw any attention from local law enforcement officers, so he shot one of the men in the head. He and Charlie buried the man that night.

The following year, Robert was called upon by the governor to kill Jesse James. Ford agreed to shoot the outlaw, so he asked his brother to initiate him formally into the gang. Jesse James was about to embark on a robbery, so Robert went to stay with him at his home, claiming that he wanted to help finalize the plans. While he was there, Ford sneaked up on the outlaw and shot him in the back. Robert was charged with murder, but he was pardoned by the governor.

Shortly thereafter, Charlie committed suicide. Robert found it difficult to cope with his brother's death, so he ran away with his lover, a dancer named Nellie Waterson. He worked for a while in P.T. Barnum's traveling freak show, but he gambled away most of his earnings.

Years later he moved to Colorado and opened a saloon. Business was good, but the area was heavily populated with outlaws. A fugitive named Ed Kelly, whom Ford had accused of stealing his ring, shot and killed him in his own saloon in 1892.

PAT GARRETT

Born: Alabama, 1850
Died: Las Cruces, Texas, 1908

When Pat Garrett was six years old, his family moved from Alabama to Louisiana. His father became a successful plantation owner, allowing young Pat to be raised with some privilege. He went to a fairly good school and was noted for his tenacity at an early age. Legend has it that he once walked through three miles of snow just to beat up a schoolmate.

The Civil War left the Garrett family in ruins. Their fortune was lost, and Pat's parents died shortly thereafter. Left with no other choice, he quit school and journeyed to Dallas County, Texas, in order to become a cowboy. For the next six years he worked hard as a cow hand, but he finally grew frustrated with his bland life and quit. He met a buffalo hunter in Denison, and he decided to become one himself. He was quite successful, but after losing all his wages in a card game in 1878, he decided it might be best to return to the life of a cow hand.

While working for a rancher in New Mexico named Pete Maxwell, Garrett be-friended one William Bonney, later to be known as Billy the Kid. Garrett, a towering six-foot-four, and Billy, a mere five-foot-seven, frequently gambled together, earn-ing the nicknames Big Casino and Little Casino. The two men both settled in Lin-coln County, but their paths went separate ways. Garrett married and had seven chil-dren, while the Kid lived the life of an outlaw. Billy's reputation grew so big that other rustlers and highwaymen from all over the West gathered in Lincoln in order to join his gang.

After running a saloon and grocery store in Lincoln for a few years, Garret was elected sheriff in 1880. He was proud of his new position, but he was shocked to learn that his first duty would be to kill his best friend. The people of Lincoln were fright-ened of all the criminals in the area, and they wanted Billy the Kid dead. He reluctantly captured his one-time gambling buddy, but the Kid escaped before his death sentence could be carried out. Garrett had to hunt him down again, and this time he killed the outlaw himself.

Pat left his position as sheriff and moved to Ulvade, Texas. He became a cattle rancher himself, and was soon elected county commissioner. He moved around for some time after that, even returning for one term as a sheriff in New Mexico, but he finally settled in El Paso, Texas, and raised horses.

In 1908, Pat Garrett was killed by Wayne Brazel, a man to whom he had rented property. When Brazel stopped paying rent, Garrett went to talk to him. Brazel opened fire, shooting him in the back and the head. Brazel was acquitted of the crime. Garrett was buried in an unmarked grave.

JAMES BUCHANAN GILLETT

Born: Austin, Texas, 1856
Died: Temple, Texas, 1937

James Gillett was raised in a middle-class household. His small amount of privilege allowed him to attend notable schools, and as a result he was trained to ride horses and shoot handguns from an early age. He ran away from home when he was seventeen, seeking adventure and excitement. For two years he found no excitement, however, forced to take a job as a cowboy in order to support himself. But he then became a Texas Ranger, and he finally found the adventure that he so dearly craved.

Gillett was a dedicated Ranger, and he was quickly promoted to the rank of corporal. In 1877, he was ordered to lead five men on a manhunt for an outlaw named Richard Dublin. The Rangers discovered that he was hiding out in a local ranch. The men surrounded the ranch, but Dublin managed to shoot his way out. It seemed as if the outlaw was going to escape, but Gillett fired one incredibly accurate shot at the fleeing man. Dublin died on the spot.

The following year Gillett was among a party of Rangers who were escorting a prisoner to trial. The Rangers came upon another outlaw named Starke Reynolds. Reynolds tried to evade them, but Gillett's riding skills were too great. Gillett managed to break away from the other Rangers and ride fast enough to catch up with the out-law. He threw Reynolds to the ground, engaged in a fist fight with him, and finally arrested him. He was promoted to sergeant for his actions.

He retired from the Texas Rangers in 1881, turning to a career in local law enforcement in El Paso, Texas. But after a few years, he resigned from this job also and became a successful cattle rancher.

JACK HELM

Born: Unknown
Died: Albuquerque, Texas, 1873

Jack Helm worked for the Sutton brothers on their ranch in Texas during the 1860s. When they began their feud with the neighboring Taylor brothers, Jack was asked to lead the Sutton Regulators, a gang of 200 men. He planned many of the bloodiest battles of that feud, and he personally killed several men with Taylor blood in their veins, or Taylor money in their pocket.

In 1869, Jack spotted several Taylor cowboys lurking about Sutton land. He opened fire on the two men, killing both of them instantly. A month later, he arranged an ambush on the Taylor ranch, pinning down several men inside. When the men finally ran out of ammunition, the Sutton Regulators stormed in and killed them.

The following year, Jack became one of the four captains of the newly organized Texas State Police. When the Kelly brothers, who

45

were related to the Taylors by marriage, paraded drunk through the streets, Jack abused his power and had the men arrested. He then led the men off with a posse of Suttons and executed them. When word of this leaked to his superiors, he was suspended from the force. After a trial several months later, he was fired altogether.

A few years later he was elected sheriff of DeWitt County. He continued to abuse his powers as a lawman, killing more and more Taylors "in the line of duty." He was killed in 1873 by two Taylors; one blew a hole through his chest with a shotgun, and the other shot him in the head with a pistol.

WILD BILL HICKOK

Born: Troy Grove, Illinois, 1837
Died: Deadwood, South Dakota, 1876

James Butler Hickok was the son of a Presbyterian deacon. He had three brothers and two sisters. His father was an ardent abolitionist who was active in the Underground Railroad. James spent many of his early years hiding with slaves on the road to freedom. He was passionate about two things as a boy: guns and the abolition of slavery. After his father's death, when James was just 15, he got into a gunfight. He ran off to Kansas to evade the law.

Kansas was in turmoil over the issue of slavery. James joined an abolitionist guerrilla organization known as the "Free State Army," and he was involved in many battles with pro-slavery forces from Missouri. Although he never enlisted in the Union Army, James fought bitterly against the South. He was a scout, a spy, and a sharpshooter. His aim became legendary, and he earned the name Wild Bill for the risks he took during battle.

In 1860, Wild Bill was mauled by a bear. Amazingly, his good looks were virtually unblemished. But he was incapacitated for many months. Soon after he recovered, he got into a gunfight with a corrupt business-man named David McCanles. He killed McCanles and injured two other men. The gunfight grew into legendary proportions through gossip. Even before he truly earned the distinction, he was known as the best shot in the world. When the Civil War ended in 1865, Wild Bill tried to settle down to a more peaceful life, but he became repeatedly embroiled in duels. His marks-manship improved further, until he was one of the most feared men in the West.

Shortly thereafter he became the Marshal of Abilene, Kansas. He loved to drink and gamble, and his very presence in town was enough to maintain law and order. He had an easy life. There was only one "incident" during his tenure as sheriff. He got into a gunfight with a drunken gambler and accidentally killed a policeman. He never again fired a gun at another man.

Wild Bill tried to cash in on his image on two occasions. He created traveling road shows in which he would demonstrate his prowess with a gun. Surprisingly, both attempts failed miserably. He simply wasn't a businessman. He then tried to win his fortune with the gold diggers of South Dakota. He settled in the town of Deadwood, where he staked several gold claims. He was shot in the back by "Broken Nose Jack" McCall during a friendly game of cards in 1876. No one knows why. McCall was hanged for the crime.

Wild Bill's relationship with Calamity Jane is still a mystery. She was a sharp shooting, tobacco chewing tomboy who apparently loved him, but there is no proof that he had affections for her. Her real name might have been Martha Jane Canary, but no one knows for sure. All that is known is that she is buried in the grave next to his.

JOHN CALHOUN PINCKNEY HIGGINS

Born: Atlanta, Georgia, 1848
Died: Kent County, Texas, 1914

John Higgins grew up in Lampasas County, Texas, moving there with his family when he was just a few months old. His parents owned a ranch, so young John grew up loving animals. His love did not extend toward all people, however, as he was indoctrinated into the Ku Klux Klan at an early age. He believed strongly in the values of that organization, and he soon rose in the ranks to become a KKK officer. His racism was extended particularly toward Native Americans, and he took great pride in the numbers he had killed. He was known to ride out on the prairies with his Winchester rifle, waiting to run across an Indian.

In his twenties, John became a rancher himself. He ran a very successful business, and his cattle drives were some of the biggest in the region. He occasionally worked in collaboration with a neighboring rancher named Horrell, but in 1873 a feud occurred between the two families.

In 1874, John found a Horrell rancher killing a Higgins cow. He killed the man, slit open the animal, and shoved his dead body inside. He then delivered the carcass to the Horrells. A few months later, John discovered another Horrell rancher on Higgins property. John shot the man twice through the stomach. Ugly fighting such as this continued for the next several years. In 1877, John entered a saloon where Merritt Horrell was having a drink. John accused the other man of tampering with his livestock, and he shot him in the head, much to the horror of the other customers. On one occasion, the two families even started a shoot-out in the middle of the town square, forcing innocent bystanders to run for their lives.

The feud finally ended the next year when Texas Rangers forced them to make peace with each other. John moved his ranch to Spur, Texas, where he lived until the time of his death.

THOMAS HODGES

Born: Tennessee
Died: Merced River, California, 1856

Hodges came from a well-to-do family, and he trained to be a doctor at an early age. He grew up in Rome, Tennessee, and he became a medical orderly in the army when the United States went to war with Mexico. After the war he opened a medical practice in Nashville, and his small business began to blossom. He then moved to California with the dream of striking it rich in the gold rush. Unfortunately, he proved to be an inept prospector, and was unable to resume his medical career as he had spent all of his money on mining equipment.

Hodges next decided to become a thief and adopted the alias Tom Bell. He was a remarkable outlaw, and he soon became a wanted man in several counties. He managed to evade the law for a few years, but he was finally caught in 1855. Hodges was sent to prison in San Francisco, but he escaped shortly thereafter with the help of several other criminals. Together they formed a gang.

The outlaws made a fortune by stealing gold from the prospectors in the area, but in 1856 their luck turned sour. Several of their robbery attempts failed, and they were forced to shoot innocent people in order to escape. On one occasion, they shot a stage driver to death who had just delivered a shipment of beer to a saloon. They found only 300 dollars in the driver's kitty. A few months later they tried to hold up another stage. This one was filled with gold and jubilant prospectors, and it was heavily armed. A gunfight occurred, resulting in heavy casualties on both sides. Incidents such as these made the gang a high priority for law enforcement officers.

Just one month later, the gang was trapped inside a cabin by a local posse comprised of lawmen and outlaws alike. The posse was victorious after many hours of shooting, and Hodges was finally brought to justice. He was allowed to write letters to his mother and his lover, and then he was hanged.

DOC HOLLIDAY

Born: Griffin, Georgia, 1852?
Died: Glenwood Springs, Colorado, 1887

John Henry Holliday was born into an aristocratic Southern household. But his days of privilege were short lived: the Civil War was destroying the economy of the South, and the Holliday fortune with it. John's mother died shortly thereafter, and his relationship with his father worsened when the man remarried. History asserts that John was sent to the Baltimore College of Dental Surgery in Maryland, but that institute has no records of a student named Holliday. It is likely that John learned dentistry through an apprenticeship, and that he merely claimed to have attended university to attain professional credibility.

Around 1870, John left Georgia in a hurry. No one knows why. Some claim that he shot several young Black men. Others claim that he suffered a bout of tuberculosis and had to move somewhere more tranquil. Holliday found himself in Dallas, where he

became one of the partners in a successful
dentistry office. It was at this time that
"Doc" turned to drinking and gambling as
everyday habits. He also started carrying a
gun with him, and he killed several men in
disputes over card games. He was arrested
and escaped at least once. In 1878 he made
his way to Dodge City and befriended
Wyatt Earp. Earp even claimed that
Holliday once saved his life, although there
is no record of this ever happening.

Very little is known of Holliday's affairs in
Dodge City. He opened a dentistry office,
but the success of his business is unknown.
Some say that he even rode with the great
Bat Masterson on a mission of mercy.
Although the two men knew each other,
there is little evidence to support any good
deeds on Doc's part. Holliday left Dodge in
quite a hurry in 1879, and that same year he
opened a saloon in Las Vegas. He was
involved in several shootings in that area, a
place heavily populated with outlaws, but
he was never arrested due to his friendship
with the sheriff. The following year he
became a card dealer in Tombstone, Ari-

zona, where he made many enemies. He was involved in the famous shoot-out at the OK Corral with Wyatt Earp, but it is unclear as to how much of the gunfight is historically accurate. Doc fled from Arizona after that.

He went as far as Denver, where he was arrested by authorities for his participation in the gunfight. Wyatt Earp discovered that Doc was in jail, and he asked Bat Masterson to arrange for his release. Masterson spoke to the governor of Colorado, and Doc soon found himself a free man.

By 1884, Doc Holliday showed visible signs of deterioration from tuberculosis. The symptoms may or may not have been due to the alleged case of approximately fourteen years earlier. But Doc did not turn to more peaceful ways. Yet again he found himself in a gunfight. He was arrested, but later acquitted.

In 1887, Holliday succumbed to tuberculosis in a hospital in Colorado.

JOHN REYNOLDS HUGHES

Born: Cambridge, Illinois, 1857
Died: Austin, Texas, 1946

John Hughes grew up in a somewhat well-to-do household in Illinois. His adventurous spirit drove him to leave home when he was just fourteen, and he made his way out west in order to work on cattle ranches. He purchased a gun on his travels, and he became a fine marksman, ensuring that no one would give him any trouble. But when he was fifteen, he got into a fight with a drunken man. The man shattered John's right hand, and it seemed as if he would never be able to shoot again. After recovering from his injury, however, John practiced long and hard to shoot with his left hand, and he eventually became an even better shot than before.

By the time he was thirty-one, John Hughes had spent over half of his life as a cowboy working on other people's ranches. He had finally managed to save up some money, and was able to buy a small ranch of his own. Eight years later, he had become a well-regarded man in the area, honest, upright, and able to defend his property. On one occasion, when several rustlers stole over 100 horses from the ranches of Hughes and his neighbors, John swore that he'd track them down. His hunt lasted nearly a year, eating up much of his money and causing him to travel literally thousands of miles on horseback. But he finally found the thieves, killed most of them, and brought back all of the stolen horses. He became a local hero.

The Texas Rangers heard of his prowess, and they asked for his assistance in tracking down vigilantes on several occasions. This infuriated local outlaws, and they put out several contracts on his life. But he always defended himself from their attacks gallantly, and he was finally asked to join the rangers, staying with them for twenty-eight years. His valor allowed him to climb the ranks quickly. After just five short years he had already attained the rank of sergeant, having imprisoned more than his fair share of outlaws. He was involved in many gunfights, his rapid left-hand draw resulting in the death or injury of many criminals. When the captain of his battalion was killed in the line of duty, Hughes was promoted and took over the position.

After leaving the Texas Rangers in 1915, Hughes retired to a more placid life, managing a local bank. He never got married. He took his own life at the age of eighty-nine.

BLACK JACK

Born: San Saba County, Texas, 1866
Died: Clayton, New Mexico, 1901

Very little is known of Thomas Ketchum's early life. In his mid-twenties he became very fond of playing cards, so he adopted the nickname "Black Jack." He was extremely strange, and he once beat himself over the head repeatedly with his pistol for no apparent reason.

As a young man, he made his living as a cowboy, but he soon discovered the pleasures to be found by stealing money from others, and he became an outlaw. He robbed banks, trains, and stagecoaches. His reputation grew steadily, until he was known by virtually every stage driver, train conductor, and bank teller in the area.

His three most famous gunfights all occurred in 1899. Once, in a saloon in Arizona, he shot two men during a dispute over a game of cards (adding new meaning to the nickname Black Jack). Both men died shortly thereafter, and Black Jack left town before he could be arrested by the local Marshal. Just ten days later, shortly after one of his most successful train heists, Ketchum and two members of his gang were attacked by a posse. The outlaws returned fire, and gunshots rang through the air for the next twelve hours. Ketchum and his gang were victorious, killing three of the lawmen, but Black Jack was badly wounded in the arm. He was arrested soon after that, his wound slowing down the gang, but he promptly escaped. Just over a month later, he returned to robbing trains. He engaged in a gunfight with the train's conductor. His arm was shot again, and he was forced to flee. He was found on the verge of death a few days later, and his arm was amputated in order to save his life.

Black Jack was tried for his crimes. He received a death sentence. Two years later, the sentence was finally carried out in Clayton, New Mexico. Witnesses say that he faced his death with courage, and he apparently gave the hangman the order to pull the lever himself.

JESSE JAMES

Born: Clay County, Missouri, 1847
Died: St. Joseph, Missouri, 1882

Jesse James's father was a Baptist minister. He had one older brother, named Frank. The boys' father died while they were very young, and their mother remarried shortly thereafter. Their stepfather was abusive, however, so this marriage did not last very long. She then married a kind doctor, and the James boys seemed as if they would finally have a peaceful life. But the Civil War broke out several years later, and the James family found itself siding with the Confederates. Union soldiers frequently stole from their household and abused members of the family, so Jesse and Frank became members of a guerrilla band fighting for the Confederates. Jesse was wounded several times, but he remained true to his cause and continued fighting as soon as he recovered.

When it became apparent that the Union would win the war, the guerrilla band evolved into a gang of thieves. They took advantage of the general lawlessness of the South, and Jesse even orchestrated the first daylight bank robbery in the history of the United States. He and his gang managed to get away with $60,000 from that heist.

Jesse orchestrated numerous robberies after that, and he clearly became the unofficial leader of the group. The robberies usually resulted in a great amount of gunplay, so it is impossible to calculate the number of deaths for which he was directly responsible. Jesse never admitted to being an outlaw, however, and he always maintained his innocence and provided solid alibis during the times when the robberies took place.

In 1873, Jesse and his gang began robbing trains. Private detectives were employed to guard the trains, and Jesse and Frank were suspected of murdering one of them. That year Jesse also got married. He soon became the father of two children, and he insisted that they be baptized. Despite his illegal and murderous activities, Jesse considered himself a devout Christian. Once he had a family, he decided that it would be best to assume an alias. He changed his name to Thomas Howard and moved to St. Joseph, Missouri, in 1881.

Jesse was planning another bank heist when he was murdered in his home by a member of his gang named Bob Ford in 1881. Ford had been commissioned by the governor to kill Jesse. Many people thought that reports of the outlaw's death were just rumors, as many men had claimed to have killed Jesse James over the years. But when Jesse's body was buried in the yard of his mother, people realized that the gang leader was truly gone. His mother let people look at the grave for twenty-five cents.

BILLY THE KID

Born: Indiana or New York, 1859
Died: Fort Sumner, New Mexico, 1881

Many people think that Billy the Kid's real name was William Bonney, but few know that that name was also an alias. His real name was Henry McCarty, and he was born in either New York or Indiana. While the Civil War was raging, his family moved from their original home to Kansas. But his father died shortly thereafter, and his older brother, Joe, became the head of the household. Joe moved them to New Mexico, where his mother remarried. She died one year later.

Billy the Kid was a short, ugly, buck-toothed man. He became a petty thief while still quite young, and he spent a short time in prison before escaping. He worked as a cowboy for several years in Eastern Arizona, but he was arrested after killing a man. He managed to escape, and made his way to New Mexico, where he was given a job in Lincoln County by a kindly rancher named John Tunstall.

For a few months it seemed as if Billy the Kid was about to settle down into a better life, but his dream was shattered when a posse killed Tunstall. He swore that he would avenge the rancher's death, and he fought back on a huge scale. Historians refer to the battles that followed as the Lincoln County War. Neither Billy the Kid and his gang nor the lawmen and their posses can truly be considered the good guys in this war. Each faction committed horrible atrocities toward the other, brutally murdering men and destroying property.

Billy the Kid managed to survive the final battle of the war, and he fled from Lincoln. He became involved in cattle rustling, as well as murdering several people. He was then pursued by lawman Pat Garrett, who ironically had been Billy the Kid's friend and gambling buddy in the past. Garrett caught Billy the Kid shortly after the pursuit began, but the outlaw killed two guards and escaped before he could face trial. Garret again set out after him, however, and this time he was able to kill the outlaw himself.

THE SUNDANCE KID

Born: Mont Claire, Pennsylvania, 1861
Died: San Vincente, Bolivia, 1908

Harry Longabaugh lived in Pennsylvania
until the age of twelve. He then moved to
Wyoming with his family. He quickly fell in
with a bad crowd, and he was forced to
serve almost three years in the Sundance
jail after stealing several horses. His time
behind bars did not reform him, however,
as he turned to more serious crime as soon
as he was released. He began robbing trains
in the early 1890s with several of his
friends, but the law began breathing down
his neck by 1892. After one botched job, two
of his friends were arrested. The Sundance
Kid barely managed to escape.

In 1896 Sundance encountered Butch
Cassidy, who had just been released from
prison. Butch wanted to form the most
notorious gang of outlaws imaginable, and
he asked Sundance to be his right-hand-
man. Always a showman, Butch named the
gang the Wild Bunch. They robbed trains

and banks, and they became folk heroes to
bored men and women back East.

Sundance helped Butch orchestrate most of
the Wild Bunch's jobs. They never worked
as well as planned, however, so the group
frequently had to split up and go into
hiding. Once the lawmen finally gave up
looking for them, they would return from
their hideouts and celebrate for months on
end with the money they had stolen. But by
1902, the lawmen of the Old West decided
they were going to put the gang away for
ever. Butch and Sundance were forced to
flee the country. Sundance brought his
mistress, who may have been either a
teacher or a prostitute, with him.

After splitting up for a few months, Butch
and Sundance reunited in Argentina and
opened a ranch. They grew tired of their
serene lives, however, so they moved to
Bolivia and began robbing trains and
banks. But in 1908 their luck turned sour.
Sundance was killed by local soldiers who
had been following them since their last job.
Butch managed to escape and returned to
the States.

BILL LEONARD

Born: Unknown
Died: Eureka, New Mexico, 1881

Bill Leonard was a respectable man who ran a jewelry business in Las Vegas, New Mexico. When his business hit hard times, he sold it and moved to Arizona, where he somehow became involved with a group of cattle rustlers and stage robbers headed by an outlaw named "Old Man" Clanton.

In 1881, Bill and several members of the gang camped out in Contention, Arizona, near a route frequently traveled by stage coaches. They had been planning a robbery for many weeks. Opportunity finally knocked when they discovered that the next stage on the route would be a Wells Fargo coach filled with over twenty-five thousand dollars. They hid out in the place along the route where they felt the coach would be the most vulnerable. When the stage reached them, they drew their guns and commanded the driver to stop. The coach was guarded by one of Wells Fargo's best private security officers, however, and he resisted the robbery, opening fire on the outlaws with a shotgun. Bill was wounded slightly in the groin, and one of his accomplices was killed. The criminals returned fire, shooting several innocent passengers. The team of horses became frightened by all of the noise, and they bolted, pulling the coach to safety. The surviving outlaws escaped.

They were finally brought to justice several months later. While attempting to rob a small store in Eureka, New Mexico, they encountered a resistant store owner, who shot Bill and one of his allies. The other criminals escaped. Bill and his friend lived just long enough to divulge the identities of their friends, and they were soon captured and put in jail.

JOHN LONG

Born: Unknown
Died: Unknown

No one knows where or when John Long was born. His name first made its mark on history in 1876, when he was still a young man. While visiting friends in Fort Griffin, Texas, Long got into an argument with several men. The argument gradually turned into a fist fight, and then very quickly into a gunfight. Long shot two men and then fled from town.

Two years later, he appeared in Lincoln County, New Mexico, where he was appointed deputy sheriff. He was involved in some serious actions during his tenure as deputy. In 1878, he was part of a posse that went out to hunt down Billy the Kid. Billy's gang ambushed the posse, however, killing the sheriff and one of his other deputies. Long killed one of the gang members with a shot from his rifle, but the others got away. A few months later, Long was sent out alone in order to arrest Billy the Kid. He managed to trace the gang's trail, and followed it to their hideout, but he found them waiting for him when he arrived. They fired a volley of bullets, killing his horse, but he managed to escape.

Long was an important figure in the Lincoln County War. He was a member of the posse that lynched John Tunstall, an incident that historians consider to be the cause of the war. The major players in this war were the lawmen of Lincoln County and Billy and his gang members. John was also involved in the final battle of the war, which lasted for four horrible days. Many men died during that battle, and much property was destroyed through arson or gunfire.

No one knows for sure how many men John Long killed. No one is even certain what became of him after the war, so it is quite likely that he retired to a calmer way of life.

CHRIS MADSEN

Born: Copenhagen, Denmark, 1851
Died: Guthrie, Oklahoma, 1944

Chris Madsen joined the Danish army
when he was just fourteen years old. He
was proud to serve his country by fighting
against the Germans. He then enlisted in
the French Foreign Legion for four years,
fighting in many battles in Algiers. He later
became a member of the French underground movement that worked toward the
defeat of Prussia. He was saddened to see
France lose to the Prussians, however, and
he was forced to take flight to America.
Despite being one of the premier law enforcement officers of the Old West, he did
not even reach American shores until he
was twenty-five years old.

As soon as he landed in New York, he
joined the 7th Cavalry, under the command
of General George Custer. But before he
ever met the famed general, Madsen was
transferred to the 5th Cavalry and sent to
Fort Hays, Kansas. Custer was killed

shortly thereafter at Little Big Horn. From Kansas, Madsen was dispatched to Wyoming to help in the battles against the Sioux. Despite his desire to further test his mettle in battle, Madsen was relegated to menial duties. Buffalo Bill frequently acted as a scout for the 5th Cavalry, and Madsen personally witnessed the famous duel in which Bill scalped the Cheyenne leader, Yellow Hand, at War Bonnet Creek.

Chris Madsen remained in the military until 1891, sometimes fighting as he hoped to, sometimes performing less dangerous duties, such as making maps. In the late 1880s, outlaws began to settle in the Oklahoma territory, making life nearly impossible for the respectable citizens of the area. William Grimes was personally requested to become the U.S. Marshal of the area by President Harrison. He became Marshal, but soon realized that he was going to need a deputy. The soldiers at Fort Reno, Oklahoma, all agreed that Chris Madsen would be perfect for the job. In 1891, Chris became Grimes' deputy after learning that he would earn almost ten times his army pay.

Chris Madsen loved the excitement of his new job. He personally hunted down some of the most dangerous men in the Old West. He even joined Teddy Roosevelt's team of Rough Riders during the Spanish-American War. On one occasion, he had to establish a courthouse in an untamed section of the territory. He single-handedly had to escort almost 50 prisoners along 190 miles of trails until he reached his destination. The night he arrived, he was almost shot when some of the prisoners escaped, but he managed to recapture them all. Madsen never had time to rest. As soon as one criminal was caught, a new one was on the loose. He faced off against train robbers, bank robbers, horse and cattle thieves, and countless other outlaws.

Despite several bouts of illness and the loss of his beloved wife, Chris Madsen remained a fighter all his life. He tried to enlist in the U.S. army during World War I, but he was too old. His son fought in his stead. He became very weak in his later years, nearly losing his eyesight and breaking a hip. He died peacefully in hospital in 1944 at the age of eighty-three.

JAMES MANNING

Born: Huntsville, Alabama, 1845
Died: Los Angeles, California, 1915

James Manning was born and raised on a plantation in the South. He had four brothers, and the five siblings were extremely loyal to each other. Firm believers in slavery and the Southern way of life, they fought on the side of the Confederacy during the Civil War. When that war was lost, they decided to protest by remaining unshaven until the South returned to its former glory.

The Manning brothers moved West in the early 1870s. They operated a successful ranch and ran many cattle drives. While on one of the drives, a man shot James' youngest brother to death. James swore revenge and pursued the man relentlessly. He finally caught up with the murderer of his brother, killing him slowly and painfully.

The brothers left Texas for a few years in order to fight with Maximillian in Mexico. When they returned they went their separate ways. James opened a saloon and tried to lead a placid life, but he quickly became embroiled in a feud with a local Marshal named Dallas Stoudenmire and his brother, Doc Cummings. One night Doc approached him in the saloon and threatened him. James tried to calm him down but was unable to, so he resorted to shooting him in the chest. Cummings dragged himself into the street, cried out in pain, and died. Stoudenmire decided to avenge the death by shooting James' brother. After finding his brother's body, James broke out his sawed-off shotgun and blew a hole through Stoudenmire's skull.

James moved to Seattle a few years later and ran another saloon. When a fire claimed that saloon, he moved elsewhere in Washington and opened another. His heart always remained in Texas, however, and he made frequent visits to his old home, where his surviving brothers remained. He then began investing in the silver and copper mines of Arizona and Nevada. His investments allowed him to retire with his wife and children in Los Angeles, where he died of cancer at the age of seventy.

BAT MASTERSON

Born: Illinois, 1853
Died: New York, New York, 1921

William Barclay Masterson was born on a farm in Illinois, but he grew up in Wichita, Kansas. He had five siblings. His father gave him his first gun at an early age, and young William spent much of his childhood practicing with the old musket. As a young man, he and his older brother Ed ran away to a life of adventure. They worked on a railroad line for several months, but when it came time to collect their pay, they were double-crossed by their boss. Ed returned home to his parents, but William stayed and worked elsewhere until he amassed enough money to buy a gun. He then returned to the boss of the railroad line and collected the money that was owed to him. He became a respected man.

Masterson then became a buffalo hunter. He was such a good shot that he killed enough buffaloes to earn 100 dollars a day. Once, while he was out hunting, he was beaten up and robbed by five Native Americans. The other hunters heard of this and rode to the safety of Dodge City. But William stayed to win his revenge. He took forty horses from the men who had robbed him, selling them in Dodge City for a huge profit.

Buffalo hunters were unpopular with the Native Americans. They were killing off the herds of animals on which the Indians relied for survival. By wiping out the buffalo, the White Man threatened to destroy the traditions and even the very existence of Native Americans. William and his fellow hunters killed countless buffalo. At the age of twenty-one, while resting in the tiny settlement of Adobe Walls, William had to use his marksmanship against human beings. The settlement was attacked by hundreds of Indians. After five days the attackers gave up, and William and the few remaining survivors returned to Dodge City.

William hated the sheriff of Dodge, Larry Deger. The two once got into a fist fight, and Masterson was sent to jail. The following year he beat Deger in the election for sheriff. He earned the nickname Bat from his tendency to hit criminals over the head with a cane. He carried this cane for good reason — he had been shot in the leg several years earlier in a gunfight over a woman. During his tenure as sheriff, Bat kept the town calm and peaceful.

Bat moved to New York in 1902 and became a sports writer for a newspaper called The *Morning Telegraph*. On only one occasion did he write an article unrelated to sports. He wrote about a murder trial that had been badly handled in upstate New York. Because of this article, Bat, the editor, and the publisher were all arrested for criminal libel. They were released with a severe scolding, and even Bat laughed at the irony of the situation. He had survived Indian attacks only to be arrested for his writing. He died in 1921, still a writer for the newspaper. He was sixty-seven.

MYSTERIOUS DAVE MATHER

Born: Connecticut, 1845
Died: Unknown

No one knows anything about the origins of "Mysterious Dave" Mather, other than the fact that he was born in Connecticut, circa 1845. Some time in his late teens or early twenties, he must have made his way out West, because he was known to be in a gang of horse rustlers in Arkansas in 1873. He became a buffalo hunter soon thereafter, but he was forced to retire from this profession after receiving a wound in the stomach during a knife fight.

In 1879, Mather switched sides of the law. After being found not guilty of criminal charges in Las Vegas, he immediately became one of the town's constables. He was actually quite dedicated to his position, and he was even involved in several gunfights in the name of law and order. But he quit the job after a few short months, hoping to strike it rich as a gold prospector. He failed as a prospector and soon found himself back in Las Vegas. Once again he switched sides of the law, and he helped arrange a jail break. His role in the plan was discovered, and he was forced to flee to Texas in order to escape the law. Shortly after arriving in Dallas, however, he was arrested for petty thievery and had to spend several months in jail.

A few years later Mysterious Dave moved to Dodge City, Kansas. He gained employment as a deputy, but the people of this town were not supportive of him. He made no effort to hide the fact that he was involved with local criminals. In 1884, Mather engaged in several shoot-outs with a rival named Tom Nixon. At one time the two had hunted buffalo together, but their relationship had turned sour in the years since. The first gunfight started after the two began arguing outside a saloon. Witnesses claim that Nixon drew his gun on Mysterious Dave and fired a shot at the deputy. The second shoot-out, which occurred three days later, erupted on exactly the same spot. Mather drew his gun first this time and killed Nixon. He was forced to flee from town, and he was never heard from again.

JEFF DAVIS MILTON

Born: Marianna, Florida, 1861
Died: Tucson, Arizona, 1947

Jeff Milton's father was the governor of Florida during the Civil War. He was raised in luxury on his family's plantation in Marianna, but much of their fortune was lost after his father died in the war. In 1877 he was forced to support himself, so he moved to Texas in order to work at his brother-in-law's store. At the age of seventeen, he decided to become completely independent, laboring as the overseer of prisoners who worked on farms.

Two years later Jeff joined the Texas Rangers. He was involved in several gunfights during his tenure as a lawman, narrowly escaping death on many occasions. Once he even had to disarm a drunken man who had just shot a fellow ranger in the face. Despite one incident of poor conduct while drunk, he was a generally well respected ranger and was promoted to the rank of corporal. After leaving the rangers, he became the manager of a store for a few months, but soon gave that up in favor of the post of deputy sheriff. He was shot once in the leg while on duty, so he decided to resign and open a saloon. He always kept a gun by his side, realizing the rowdiness of some of his patrons.

A few years later he found himself working on a ranch in New Mexico. He decided to return to law enforcement, taking a position as deputy sheriff. His many years as a lawman could not prepare him for his duties in New Mexico, however. On one occasion he was even mauled by a grizzly bear. A few years later he became a border patrol officer, working on the 900 miles of border between Mexico and Arizona.

Milton then became a fireman in Tucson for several years, later accepting the position of chief of police in El Paso. He was shot in the arm while guarding a train, forcing him to retire permanently from law enforcement. After failing to make his fortune by investing in oil wells in California and Texas, he joined the Immigration Service. He worked hard until his retirement in 1930. He died 17 years later at the age of eighty-five.

WILLIAM MINER

Born: Jackson, Kentucky, 1847
Died: Milledgeville, Georgia, 1913

William Miner grew up in a dysfunctional household. His mother, a teacher, was a battered and emotionally abused woman. His father was an alcoholic who ran out on the family when William was just ten years old. The young boy then fell in with a bad crowd, and by the age of thirteen he had run away from home.

In order to support himself, he took various odd jobs on ranches, slowly moving farther and farther west. This heavy labor made him grow big and strong, and he intimidated most people around him. He arrived in California in the early 1860s, and his success at delivering messages through hostile terrain inspired him to run a mail service. But despite all his efforts, the service failed, as larger corporations could cover a wider area than he was able to. William then turned to a life of crime. In 1869, he was arrested during a failed attempt at robbing a stage coach, and he was

sentenced to fifteen years in prison. He
served ten years of his sentence before
being released, after which he returned to
his life of crime. He began robbing trains
with an old friend of his, and the pair were
extremely successful. A posse soon formed
to hunt them down. William barely managed to escape by the skin of his teeth, but
his friend was captured and hanged.

Miner's reputation as an outlaw had grown
so big that he was forced to leave the country. He moved to Europe, where he became
part of a slavery ring that sold Turkish
women to harems. He eventually returned
to America, resumed his career as a stage
and train robber, was caught again, and
spent another ten years behind bars.

Two years after his release, he was caught
robbing a stage. He fled to Canada, but the
authorities in that country decided to throw
him in jail. He managed to escape by dig-
ging a tunnel, and he returned to the U.S.
But his reputation had not been forgotten,
and he was arrested soon after he arrived.
He spent the rest of his life in jail, attempting to escape at least three times.

JOHN MORCO

Born: Unknown
Died: Ellsworth, Kansas, 1873

Very little is known about the early years of
John Morco. He was an uneducated alcoholic who spent most of his childhood and
young adult years in California. After
killing four unarmed men in a drunken
rage, he left the state and arrived in
Ellsworth, Kansas. He boasted about his
prowess with a gun, and exaggerated
greatly the number of lives he had taken.
But his reputation soon spread around the
small town, and he was asked to become a
local deputy. He eagerly accepted the post.

Morco continued to abuse the bottle during
his tenure as a lawman. He beat his wife on
a regular basis, and he once killed a man
who tried to stop him. His drinking even
resulted in the death of the local sheriff. He
once got drunk with a gambler named John
Sterling. Another gambler, Ben Thompson,
insisted that Sterling pay off an I.O.U. from
an old poker game, but Sterling refused. He

then punched Thompson in the face. Thompson armed himself and sought out the two drunken men. He challenged them to a duel, and guns were about to be drawn when the sheriff arrived to break things up. Thompson was about to surrender his weapon when Morco began firing. Ben returned the fire, accidentally killing the sheriff. Although Thompson was never charged with murder, Morco was forced to leave the police force.

The following month, Morco decided to leave town. He took several stolen weapons with him. He was apprehended a few counties away, and the guns were returned. But John Morco managed to escape, and he returned to Ellsworth. He was shot through the head by the new sheriff when he failed to give up the gun he was carrying.

BURT MOSSMAN

Born: Aurora, Illinois, 1867
Died: Unknown

Burt Mossman was the only son of a farmer. He moved to Missouri with his parents at the age of six, where they had bought a new farm. When he was nine, the family moved again, leaving behind the farm life in favor of that of townspeople. Six years later they moved one last time, finally settling down in New Mexico. Burt loved the open plains, and especially the horses and cattle. He took a job as a cowboy as soon as his parents would allow it. He was so reliable in his duties that he was promoted to the manager of a huge ranch by the time he was twenty-one.

Mossman was a respectable man, and his life as a manager was free of incident except for one occasion. While delivering some livestock to Mexico, he got into a fight with a local soldier in a bar. The soldier challenged him to a duel. Mossman accepted the challenge, and he wounded the soldier badly in the shoulder with his shot. He was promptly arrested for attempted murder, but he was able to escape from a Mexican prison four weeks later.

In 1897, Mossman moved to Arizona in order to manage a two million-acre ranch. Arizona was full of cattle rustlers at the time, so most of his duties involved trying to apprehend them. He realized that he would have to become a member of the local law enforcement agency in order to have enough clout to stop the rustlers, so he got himself appointed to the post of deputy sheriff. Once, while out patrolling the plains, Mossman was shot at by cattle thieves. Their bullets came so close that one actually grazed his nose, and another ripped through his saddle horn.

Mossman was a great businessman. He invested in opera houses and local stores, eventually turning a huge profit. He was so well respected that he was the first choice to lead the Arizona Rangers, a group of law-men who hunted down the state's most notorious outlaws. He left the Rangers in 1902 and retired with his wife.

FLAT NOSE

Born: Prince Edward Island, Canada, 1871
Died: Castle Gate, Utah, 1900

Although he was born in Canada, George Curry spent his childhood in Chadron, Nebraska. When he reached his late teens, he moved West in an attempt to satisfy his craving for adventure. He earned a job as a horse breaker, but he was soon kicked in the face by one of the unbroken animals. His colleagues began calling him Flat Nose, and he bitterly left his job in order to take up a life of crime.

He joined a famous gang known as the Wild Bunch, and he began a career of holding up trains and stages. The Wild Bunch were not known for their precise planning abilities, however, and their robbery attempts were frequently unsuccessful. In 1897, while on the run from one of their failures, Curry and two other members of the gang, one of whom was the Sundance Kid, found themselves in Montana. One night, while they were camping out and trying to make plans for another train robbery, they were surrounded by local law enforcement officers. The three outlaws were injured in the ensuing gun-fight, and they were sent to jail. But they managed to escape shortly thereafter.

In 1899 the three men staged a successful train robbery, stealing over $8000 worth of gold from the cargo hold. They rode into Wyoming, and again they found them-selves surrounded by a posse while camp-ing out. This time, however, the outlaws won the gunfight and escaped to freedom.

The following year Curry had to resume his job as a horse breaker. It is unclear as to how he lost all of the money he had stolen. He decided to steal some of the horses from the ranch where he worked, so his boss organized a posse to hunt him down. They soon found his trail, and they shot him in the head. He lived long enough to find a hiding place, but the posse discovered his body several hours later. He was such a famous outlaw by that time that local businessmen made wallets out of the skin from his chest and sold them at a hefty price.

BAZ OUTLAW

Born: Georgia, 1855
Died: El Paso, Texas, 1894

Baz Outlaw grew up in a wealthy home in Tennessee. He was an extremely well-read man, the result of his exceptional liberal arts education. His manners were impeccable; he always treated everyone, even his most dreaded enemies, with courtesy. He began drinking at an early age, however, and by his twenties it had become a huge stumbling block in his life, destroying a promising career, as well as several important relationships.

He ran away from his family at the age of thirty, possibly fleeing the law after killing a man during a drunken rage. He joined the Texas Rangers, and he was well liked, but his drinking again proved to be a problem. Once, while in Mexico, he got into an argument with a Mexican man. Extremely drunk, Outlaw produced his pistol and shot the man before his fellow rangers could stop him. The man died, and Outlaw and his friends had to flee the scene. That same year he was discovered drunk by a superior officer, and he was kicked out of the Texas Rangers for good.

He maintained a career in law enforcement, however. Through connections that his wealth and distinction could provide, Outlaw was appointed Deputy U.S. Marshal in El Paso. His superiors knew that he was a drunk, but they neglected to warn him of the dangers he was putting himself into by drinking, as they feared he could make them lose their jobs. In 1894, while in a drunken stupor, Outlaw began shooting through windows in El Paso. When he was confronted by a Texas Ranger and a local deputy, he shot the former through the head and the latter through the leg. But the deputy managed to fire a shot through Outlaw's chest before he went down, killing him instantly.

COMMODORE PERRY OWENS

Born: East Tennessee, 1852
Died: Seligman, Arizona, 1919

Owens was born on a farm in Tennessee, the son of a violent man and his abused wife. The family moved to Indiana while he was just a small boy, and it is there that he grew up. Tiring of his father's harsh ways, Owens left home while still a teenager and made his way to Texas, where he got a job as a cowboy. He then found work as a buffalo hunter, traveling as far west as Apache County in the Territory of Arizona. By the age of thirty he had become a successful buffalo hunter and a crack shot. He also burst with pride, taunting the Native Americans to scalp him of his beautiful long hair. He carried as many as five different guns with him at one time, each useful in different situations, just in case he ran into any Indians. Legend has it that the Navajos actually held a council about Owens; they decided that he must be charmed as they had failed to kill him after so many years.

Owens later moved to Cottonwood Seep, where he opened a horse ranch and ran cattle. His horses were of such a fine stock that Owens was continually attacked by both Native Americans and outlaws who hoped to steal some of them. He successfully defended himself for years and years, never relying on official law enforcement as the nearest sheriff was located over 200 miles away. Due to ever shifting boundaries, Owens soon found his ranch situated on Mexican soil, and the mountains and plains around him became the battlefields for Texans and Mexicans who seemed bent on destroying each other. The war escalated and became more personal; both Texans and Mexicans began to carry out personal vendettas in honor of their fallen comrades. Owens became embroiled in some of these personal battles, and it is said that he single-handedly took on as many as eighty Mexicans.

The Texans eventually regained control of the area, pushing the Mexicans back to the mountains, and a town named Holbrook began to flourish when a railway line was built through the area. This town began to attract many unsavory elements who arrived on the train, and blood began to be shed. Further boundary-shuffling resulted in Holbrook becoming the seat of a new county, and Owens was named the sheriff in recognition of his past bravery. One of his first duties was to bring the Hash Knife War, a feud between cowboys from Montana and Texas, to an end. Owens managed to end the feud, but not before 15 cowboys had been senselessly killed.

Owens' most famous deed was the slaying of four of Arizona's most notorious outlaws — jurisdiction and borders had never really mattered to him. The four men were members of the Graham-Blevins gang, and news of the gruesome gunfight reached as far as San Francisco.

In 1902, Owens' career of excitement came to a happy end. He got married, moved to Seligman, and opened a saloon. Very little is known of the last days of his life.

HENRY AMOS PLUMMER

Born: 1830?
Died: Bannack City, Idaho, 1863

Henry Amos Plummer is a mystery to historians. He was probably born some time around 1830. He may have been born in Maine, Wisconsin, California, or any of twenty other places, including England. He may have been short and well-groomed, or he may have been tall and unkempt. There are so many conflicting reports about him that it is impossible to know which descriptions are correct.

In 1856, two men escaped from a jail in Nevada City, California. A posse formed to capture them, and one of the men on the posse was Henry Plummer. The posse had to separate in order to cover as much ground as possible, and when they all regrouped at nightfall, they noticed that Plummer, the sheriff, and his deputy were missing. They went out again and discovered the bodies of the two lawmen, and they assumed that Plummer had been killed as well. But Plummer rode back into town two days later, claiming to have been searching for the fugitives. The locals rewarded his courage by making him sheriff. He performed his duties well, and he was popular in town. But word soon leaked that he was having an affair with a married woman. The woman's husband came after him, and he was forced to shoot the jealous man in self-defense. He was sentenced to ten years in jail in San Quentin.

Plummer was released after only nine months due to the popular outcry in his favor from the townspeople. He returned their generosity and sympathy by storming back into town and killing a man. A few weeks later, he tried to rob a Wells Fargo stagecoach, but charges could not be filed against him for either crime due to lack of evidence. He then killed another man in a brothel. He was thrown into jail for this last crime, but he was able to escape.

Gold was discovered in Idaho in 1860, attracting a wave of prospectors. Plummer was one of the men who arrived in hopes of winning his fortune. When he realized that he could not earn his living honestly, he returned to a life of crime, becoming the ringleader of a gang of criminals. A devastating crime wave began shortly thereafter. He managed to con the people of Bannack City, Idaho into thinking that he was the only chance for law and order, and he soon became sheriff of the county. More gold was discovered several months later, and more prospectors began piling into the area. In order to make the incoming miners feel like they were in a safe environment, Plummer erected a gallows in the town square. But he secretly added more and more men to the underground ranks of his outlaw gang. The crimes in the area continued, but the sheriff never arrested anybody, so he began to lose popular support. During that time, a well-liked miner was killed. The prime suspects were two of Plummer's deputies, who confessed to being in his gang of outlaws during their trial.

After the trial came to an end, a lynch mob was formed. They captured Plummer and hanged him on the very gallows that he had built. Witnesses say that he died like a "coward."

JIM RILEY

Born: 1853
Died: Unknown

Very little is known of Jim Riley, except for his role in one of the most famous gunfights of the Old West. Riley first rode into the town of Newton, Kansas, in 1871, and he soon befriended a rowdy railroad worker named Mike McCluskie. After McCluskie killed a gambler from Texas, several other Texans swore they would avenge his death.

Mike knew that the Texans would come to get him, but he wasn't scared. He went about his business as usual, milling about the bad parts of Newton. On the night of August 20, 1871, Mike spent the night drinking in a saloon called the Alamo. When it closed at midnight, he went over to Perry Tuttle's Place, another saloon that was still open. Riley refused to leave his friend in this time of crisis; he stood watch at the entrance to the saloon.

One hour after Mike arrived in the saloon,

one of the cowboys from Texas made his presence known. He walked over to Mike's table and shot him in the neck. The railroad worker tried to defend himself, but he could not get off a shot before being hit two more times, once in the leg and once in the back. More of the Texas cowboys rose to their feet in order to make sure that no one would fire on their ally. An innocent local attempted to break up the trouble, and the Texans shot him in the head. Two of McCluskie's friends began shooting at the Texans, but they were both killed almost immediately. Riley, still standing by the entrance, locked the door and began shooting at the group of Texans. When the dust settled, six of them were dead, and the rest were attempting to flee. This incident has been recorded in history as Newton's General Massacre.

JOHN RINGO

Born: Unknown
Died: Turkey Creek Canyon, Arizona, 1882

Very little is known of the notorious John Ringo. Some historians consider him to be one of the best gunfighters of the day, while others consider him inconsequential. Some claim that his true name was Ringgold, while others feel that it was simply Ringo. He was born some time around 1850, probably on the East Coast, and he most likely attended a university.

He made his way to the West some time during the late 1860s, and he may have even fought in the Texas range wars. He was imprisoned at least once, where he befriended several bad men. Upon release, Ringo moved even further West, eventually arriving in Arizona.

Ringo had a love-hate relationship with the town in which he lived. He was well respected, and he was even appointed deputy sheriff for a few years, but at the same time it was common knowledge that he was a cattle rustler. During the day he worked alongside sheriffs and marshals, but at night he spent his time with such memorable outlaws as the Clanton brothers. He had probably studied British literature at a university, as he liked to impress townsfolk with recitals of Shakespeare. But he drank far too much, which led to several incidents. Once, while in a saloon, for example, he insisted that the man next to him have another drink. The man refused, so Ringo beat him over the head with his gun and slashed his throat. On another occasion, one of Wyatt Earp's brothers was shot and seriously wounded while standing outside a saloon. Witnesses claim that they saw Ringo exiting the saloon from the rear, incredibly drunk and carrying a rifle; it was well known that Ringo hated the Earps.

John Ringo died in 1882. His body was found in Turkey Creek Canyon. He had left town two weeks before, drunker than anyone had ever seen him. His death was considered a suicide, as there was a bullet lodged in his head, but the coroner's report also noted that he had been scalped.

BUCKSHOT ROBERTS

Born: Unknown
Died: Blazer's Mill, New Mexico, 1878

Not much is known about the earliest years of Andrew Roberts. He was probably born and raised in the South, and he had a self-created reputation as an outlaw. He spread rumors that he had escaped from jail, served with the Texas Rangers, and robbed numerous trains. It is therefore impossible to figure out exactly who this man really was.

Roberts went by the name Buckshot because he carried a shotgun with him wherever he went. He walked with a limp which he claimed was the result of being wounded by a fellow Texas Ranger. He also had very poor control over the motor muscles in his arm; he was unable to raise his shotgun above his waist, claiming that this was the result of another gunfight.

Buckshot was a key figure in the Lincoln County War. He was among the men who killed rancher John Tunstall. Billy the Kid swore revenge for this incident, as Tunstall was the man who had offered him the hope of leaving his life of crime. Billy formed a group known as the Regulators with the intentions of hunting down every man on the posse that had killed Tunstall.

The first man killed by the Regulators was Sheriff William Brady, the leader of the posse. Rewards were posted for the members of the Regulators. Buckshot decided to hunt them down; he wanted the reward money, and he also wanted to sleep peacefully at night with the knowledge that they could not harm him. While trailing them, Roberts accidentally stumbled upon them. Several members of the group ordered him to surrender and drop his weapon, but he refused. Charlie Bowdre shot his pistol at him, and Buckshot returned fire; Bowdre's shot tore through Roberts' chest, but Buckshot's bullet bounced off a metal plate in Charlie's belt. The bullet then struck George Coe, another Regulator, in the hand. Buckshot fell to the ground, and died several hours later.

LAFAYETTE SHADLEY

Born: Unknown
Died: Stillwater, Oklahoma, 1893

Shadley spent his entire life in the small Oklahoma town of Stillwater. He was one of its most respected citizens, and he was proud to wear the badge of Marshal. It is unclear, however, if he was born there, or if his family had moved from elsewhere in the country. He was one of the most famous lawmen of the West during the early 1890s, eager to take on some of the most vicious gangs in the area.

Shadley was involved in two famous gunfights. The first occurred in 1892, when he encountered a bank robber and horse thief named "Dynamite Dick" Clifton. Clifton opened fire on the Marshal, and Shadley returned fire, hitting the outlaw in the neck. Clifton escaped, and it is unknown to this day whether he survived or not.

The second famous gunfight was to be his last. In 1893, the outlaw Bill Doolin and his gang stormed into town. Shadley called for reinforcements before he moved in on the men, who were busy disturbing the peace. Over twenty lawmen soon arrived in the town, and the air became thick with tension. The peace officers tried to enter the town as covertly as possible. The first shot was fired by a lawman named Dick Speed. Speed was killed by a shot fired by a sniper from the second-story window of a hotel. Doolin and his other gang members began shooting recklessly, and a tremendous gunfight ensued that seemed to engulf the entire town. The gang's first shots killed a young boy and a horse. The outlaws ran for cover in a stable.

Shadley began shooting at the gang through the front of the stable. Several of the outlaws stormed through the front on horseback; they were killed almost instantly, but they were merely diversions. Doolin escaped through the back. Shadley pursued Doolin, but he was shot three times in the chest. The outlaw escaped to safety. Four other lawmen died with Shadley that day.

JOHN SLAUGHTER

Born: Sabine Parish, Louisiana, 1841
Died: Douglas, Arizona, 1922

John Slaughter's parents were ranchers. They had moved to Texas when John was just three months old. He grew up on the ranch, learning how to shoot and ride with great proficiency. He also developed a hatred for Native Americans during his youth, as the ranch was frequently attacked by Apache. When the Civil War began, the Texas Rangers recruited local men to fight Indians, and John gladly signed on.

When the war ended, he married a woman and bought his own ranch in a neighboring county. Although this ranch grew large and successful, Slaughter decided to abandon it and move to Arizona in 1878. His wife died of smallpox on the way.

He found another wife in 1879, and slowly began building an empire for himself. Over the next five years he managed to amass over 65,000 acres of land for a cattle ranch.

He was generally well respected by locals and lawmen, but he was suspected of having killed several men in nearby New Mexico during the Lincoln County War. Slaughter invested in the future of his land, commissioning complex irrigation systems, hiring dozens of cowboys, and even employing over thirty families to harvest crops. He was never lenient on local rustlers, and he personally executed dozens of them. This attitude earned him the admiration of his neighboring ranchers, who elected him the sheriff.

Slaughter was an active sheriff. Over the next ten years, he not only put away most of the rustlers, but he also imprisoned or killed virtually every other outlaw crazy enough to rear his head. Slaughter's private business boomed during these years, and he even began shipping cattle to California. He finally retired from law enforcement, and he played with the idea of going into politics. He soon discovered his hatred for politics after serving as a local official, however, so he focused his attention on his ranch. He died of old age when he was 80 years old.

TOM SMITH

Born: New York, New York, 1840?
Died: Abilene, Kansas, 1870

Very little is known of the early life of Thomas James Smith, the Marshal of Abilene in the years prior to Wild Bill Hickok. He came from New York, and was born around 1840. He was of Irish descent, and he might have been a boxer. He was apparently very quiet, and avoided using his gun whenever possible.

Smith had been a Marshal in Wyoming prior to arriving in Abilene, and he had made quite a reputation for himself. Once, while protecting a friend, he went on a shooting spree. He didn't kill anyone, but he received a serious wound. Much to everyone's amazement, he recovered from his injuries, and a rumor spread that he was bullet-proof. In the mid-1860s, Abilene became bustling and prosperous as one of the stops on the wearisome Chisolm Trail, the route by which cattle were shipped from Texas to the east. But such growth had its drawbacks; the cowboys who drove the cattle were a ragged band of men, and they often made trouble in the town in much the same way that modern navy seamen do when they have shore leave. It was such a dangerous job trying to keep these rowdy men under control that no one wanted to be Marshal of Abilene.

Then one day Tom Smith arrived in town. Only a few weeks earlier the cowboys had actually torn down the town's jail. The mayor warned Smith of the dangers of Abilene, but Tom took the job of Marshal anyway. Tom's first decree in order to maintain law and order was that all visitors had to hand their guns in to the marshal's office. He slowly made the cowboys comply with his wishes, beating up, rather than shooting, anyone who begged to differ.

On one occasion a wrong-doer even tried to set fire to a saloon in order to prevent himself from getting beaten up. All that happened was that several of his friends were trampled when everyone tried to escape from the saloon; Smith still arrested the man, and he beat him even harder for the jeopardy in which he had put everyone.

Tom Smith was killed tragically in 1870, at the approximate age of thirty. Andrew McConnell, a man who lived on the outskirts of town, killed a neighbor during a fight over the rights to some cattle. Tom Smith and the county sheriff went to McConnell's place to arrest him for the crime. A gunfight ensued in which Smith was wounded seriously and McConnell was wounded lightly in the hand. The sheriff ran, fearing for his life. Smith and McConnell began to struggle on the floor, the Marshal failing to notice that his adversary had brought a friend with him. The friend picked up an ax and cut Smith's head off. Tom Smith received the funeral of a hero.

JOHN A. SPRADLEY

Born: Simpson County, Mississippi, 1853
Died: Nacogdoches, Texas, 1940

Young John Spradley was the oldest son of a farmer. He had eight brothers and sisters. At the age of eighteen, he got into a gun fight when two youths opened fire on him. John was unhurt, but his brother received a serious wound in the hip and a light wound in the scalp. Spradley killed the two youths with his father's pistol, and he was forced to leave town the next day in order to evade the law.

Spradley ran as far as Texas, where he took a job on his uncle's farm. He then took a job at a mill. Unaware of his past, the residents of Nacogdoches County found him to be an upstanding young man. He worked hard, had many friends, and did not touch a gun for nine years. In 1880 he accepted the position of deputy sheriff, and he was so well respected that he was promoted to sheriff just one year later.

Spradley was involved in three memorable gunfights during his tenure as sheriff. In 1884, he arrested a drunken man in a saloon. The man's brother protested the arrest, and Spradley threatened to arrest him too if he did not return home immediately. The man's brother seemed to back down, but he suddenly whirled around with his pistol drawn and fired a shot that drove a bullet through Spradley's body. Spradley returned fire, taking down his assailant. The sheriff's wounds healed with time, and he was able to resume his duties. In 1887, he was attacked by a young man in a meat market. The man fired at him, but the bullet bounced off of a metal plate that the sheriff sometimes wore beneath his shirt for protection. Spradley then disarmed the man and arrested him. Five years later, he was attacked by a saloon owner on a train. The man tried to escape through a window when the sheriff pulled a gun on him, so Spradley shot the man.

Spradley led an active life until the time of his death in 1940, spending his final years as a farmer and a saloon owner, and even dabbling in politics.

BILL TILGHMAN

Born: Fort Dodge, Iowa, 1854
Died: Cromwell, Oklahoma, 1924

William Matthew Tilghman, born on July 4, was almost killed by an Indian arrow at the age of six months. When he was two, his family relocated to a farm in Kansas. The next six years of his life were relatively carefree. But then, at the age of eight, he became the man of the house when his father and older brother were called to fight in the Civil War. Bill minded the farm well during their absence, as well as becoming a great hunter in order to provide meat for his mother and sisters.

A few years after his father and brother returned from the War, Bill ventured West. His early exploits almost resulted in his death on four occasions. Once he was almost killed by a Cheyenne war party. Once he got caught in a blizzard and his horse succumbed to the cold. Once he got thrown from a bucking horse while work-ing as a horse breaker. And once he caught severe pneumonia.

An ace sharpshooter, Tilghman moved to Dodge City and became a Buffalo hunter. Legend says that he once shot a buffalo from a mile away. After giving up buffalo hunting, Tilghman turned to a career in law enforcement. In 1878 he became Bat Masterson's deputy sheriff. He was a well liked and respected man, and he took his job seriously. He rarely found it necessary to draw his gun on a criminal as he was usually able to overcome any adversary with a good, solid punch. Four years later, he was appointed the Marshal of Dodge City. He stayed there until 1889, preserving the peace in the face of some of the most dangerous outlaws of the Old West.

Bill was finally lured away from Dodge by an offer to become Deputy U.S. Marshal of Oklahoma, a position that allowed him to better provide for his family. Oklahoma was a dangerous area of the country. It had only recently been officially settled, so there were plenty of outlaws who had been taking refuge in the area between jobs. It was Bill's duty to deal with such men by any means necessary. Tilghman's arch-enemy during this time was an outlaw named Bill Doolin. Doolin had such respect for Tilghman that he once stopped one of his own men from shooting the Marshal in the back.

At the turn of the century, Bill Tilghman made a career move into politics. He was elected to the Oklahoma senate, and he even came to know President William Howard Taft. Shortly thereafter, he made a semi-documentary film about his exploits called *The Passing of the Oklahoma Outlaws*. It became a big hit in Los Angeles, the center of the budding film industry. In 1922 he was ousted from the Oklahoma government when he refused to support members of the Ku Klux Klan. The Klan was a dominant force in Oklahoma early in the century.

Bill Tilghman died in 1924 when he was shot by Wiley Lynn, a government prohibition enforcement officer who had become involved in a narcotics ring.

TOM TUCKER

Born: Unknown
Died: Texas

Tom Tucker was involved in several feuds during his lifetime. He fought in the Pleasant Valley War — a large feud in Arizona — and he was a member of a group of fighters named the Hash Knife outfit. This group was involved in some of the bloodiest battles of the feud.

In 1877, Tucker and seven other members of the Hash Knife outfit hunted down a rancher named Jim Tewksbury. They pinned the man down in his house and called for his surrender. He responded by opening fire on them. Four of Tucker's companions were hit by the shower of bullets, two fatally. Tucker escaped the first volley unharmed, but when he began to approach the house, he was shot in the chest. The bullet went completely through his body. He fell to the ground and managed to crawl to safety before passing out. That night it began to rain, and when he woke up he found himself being nursed in the home of one of his friends. After several painful weeks, he finally began to recover.

Tucker then moved to New Mexico and became a cowboy for a rancher named Oliver Lee. Lee was embroiled in feuds with several other local ranchers, so Tucker became involved in the fighting. He captured a man who was suspected of killing one of Lee's friends, shooting him in the head. When the man's father discovered what had happened, he hunted down Lee and Tucker and began shooting at them. They returned fire. In all, over 100 bullets were fired, but no one was hurt. The following year, Tucker accidentally killed several Chinese railroad workers who got caught in a crossfire between him and a rancher. He fled town, and later became a sheriff's deputy.

Tucker did very little as a law enforcement officer. He handled several arrests, but he was not involved in any more shoot-outs. Nobody knows how many years he labored as a peace officer. All that is known is that he faded into anonymity and died somewhere in Texas.

BEN TURNER

Born: Unknown
Died: Lincoln County, New Mexico, 1873

Ben Turner first made his mark on history when he arrived in Lincoln County, New Mexico. He was hired as a cowboy by the Horrell brothers, and he fought on their side when a feud ignited between them and their neighbors, the Higgins brothers. The feud started when the two families began arguing over claims to cattle and land.

In 1873, state police came into town in order to arrest Clint Barkley, another of the Horrell's hired hands. The Horrells were fiercely loyal to their employees, so they decided to defend him from the law. Turner accompanied the Horrells to a saloon in the town center. They waited for the lawmen to enter, and then proceeded to riddle them with bullets. Two of the Horrells were wounded, but Turner managed to escape unharmed.

A few days later, two of the Horrell brothers were thrown in jail for what had transpired in the saloon. Turner, Barkley, and the remaining Horrells immediately rode into town in order to spring them from jail. Despite heavy gunfire, they managed to break down the jail doors. Barkley was wounded in the side, but Turner again escaped without injury. He shot several police officers before fleeing with the gang.

Ben Horrell was killed in a brawl with several Mexican men a few months later. Turner hunted down the men in order to avenge his death, but he did not count on the resistance that they showed him. The men shot him and left him to die in the street.

CHAUNCEY BELDEN WHITNEY

Born: 1842
Died: Ellsworth, Kansas, 1873

Very little is known of the early years of Chauncey Whitney. He was definitely born in 1842, but no one is sure where. He was one of the founders of the town of Ellsworth, Kansas, which grew very quickly after a railroad line had been established through it. He served as the town's first sheriff, and even orchestrated the construction of its first jail. He was the commander of a militia that was organized to repel attacks by Native Americans; for several years, he was literally Ellsworth's first line of defense. He even participated in the famed Battle of Beecher Island, a skirmish in which many Native Americans were killed.

His career in law enforcement came to an ironic end just six years after it began. One of his best friends was a man named Billy Thompson. Thompson had a shady past, but no one ever asked him about it as he seemed to be such a kind and loyal man. One of Thompson's friends had gotten into a brawl with two men over a game of cards. Thompson heard about the brawl, and, though very drunk, he rushed to his friend's assistance. When Sheriff Whitney came to break up the brawl, Thompson was calm at first. The sheriff seemed to have everything in hand when Thompson exploded and began shooting recklessly. He almost killed a couple that was passing by with the first round from his shotgun, and then he accidentally shot Whitney with the second round.

Whitney was badly injured and realized that he was going to die. He called out for his wife, and he also insisted that his friend should not be punished as his injury was an accident. He died three days later, after suffering terrible pain from the wound.

ZIP WYATT

Born: Indiana, 1863
Died: Enid, Oklahoma, 1895

Nathaniel "Zip" Wyatt was born on a farm in Indiana, but he moved to Oklahoma with his parents while he was still very young. Oklahoma was not a good atmosphere in which to grow up, as it was so heavily populated with outlaws. His brother took to carrying a gun at an early age, and he was eventually killed in a gunfight. This incident shattered Zip emotionally, as he loved his older brother dearly. Zip tried to follow in his footsteps. He began carrying a gun, and he robbed several stores and trains. He even killed a few men.

In 1891, in a drunken stupor, Zip rode through the town of Mulhall, Oklahoma, brandishing his shotgun. He shot out several store windows. The townsfolk decided they were not going to put up with him, so several store owners shot back. He quickly galloped out of town, wounding a few people with his gun as he left.

Three years later, Zip was involved in a particularly vicious murder. He broke into a store with several friends. When the store owner resisted, they shot him in the arm. But the man kept fighting, so they finally shot him to death in front of his family. Within the next few months, Zip was involved in at least two more similarly brutal murders, in which a train station telegraph operator and a county treasurer were killed. Hearing that local lawmen were hot on his trail, he went to Kansas, where he killed Sheriff Andrew Balfour in a gunfight.

Zip fled to Indiana the following year, but he was apprehended by lawman Chris Madsen. He was sent to jail but escaped a few months later. A posse was organized to track him down; they found him asleep in a cornfield in Skeleton Creek, Oklahoma, and they shot him to death.

THOMAS COLEMAN YOUNGER

Born: Lee's Summit, Missouri, 1844
Died: Lee's Summit, Missouri, 1916

Thomas Younger had thirteen brothers and
sisters. They were raised by their father in
Lee's Summit, Missouri, on a rather large
plot of land that was tended by slaves.
Despite keeping slaves, however,
Younger's father sided with the Union
during the Civil War. He actively fought
against the South, and he demanded that
his sons do the same. But when his father
was shot to death in 1862, Thomas finally
let his true feelings be known; he joined the
Confederate army. By the age of eighteen,
Thomas' military prowess had resulted in
his appointment as a Confederate officer.

Younger's commission allowed him to
travel throughout the South and Old West.
He was in Los Angeles when the Civil War
came to an end, and he eagerly returned
home. Upon arrival, he met up with an old
army buddy of his named Frank James.
Frank was delighted to see his old friend,
and the two men went out drinking with

each other. Frank's brother, Jesse, accompanied them. Frank and Jesse had big plans to form a band of outlaws, and Thomas was very interested. He volunteered his services as well as those of his brothers. Their first bank robbery was an unqualified success, and the James-Younger gang was formed.

Although Jesse was the unofficial leader of the gang, he and Thomas always argued, forcing Younger to pull off several jobs on his own. The James-Younger gang was feared by nearly every honest banker and stage driver in the Missouri area. They pulled off hundreds of robberies, and many more were falsely attributed to them. The law was always on their tail, and the Younger brothers were occasionally forced to flee the state until things calmed down. But in 1876, after a bitter gunfight in which Thomas received eleven wounds, he and his brothers surrendered to a posse.

They were sentenced to life in prison, but Thomas was released in 1903 after both of his brothers had died behind bars. He worked as an insurance salesman for a short time after that. He died in 1916.